As the population increased on the east coast of North America, the Europeans moved westward invading the land of the Native Americans.

The Native Americans resisted the Europeans by both peace treaties and warfare.

The Europeans mainly won
battles because they had
more weapons and many
times broke peace treaties.

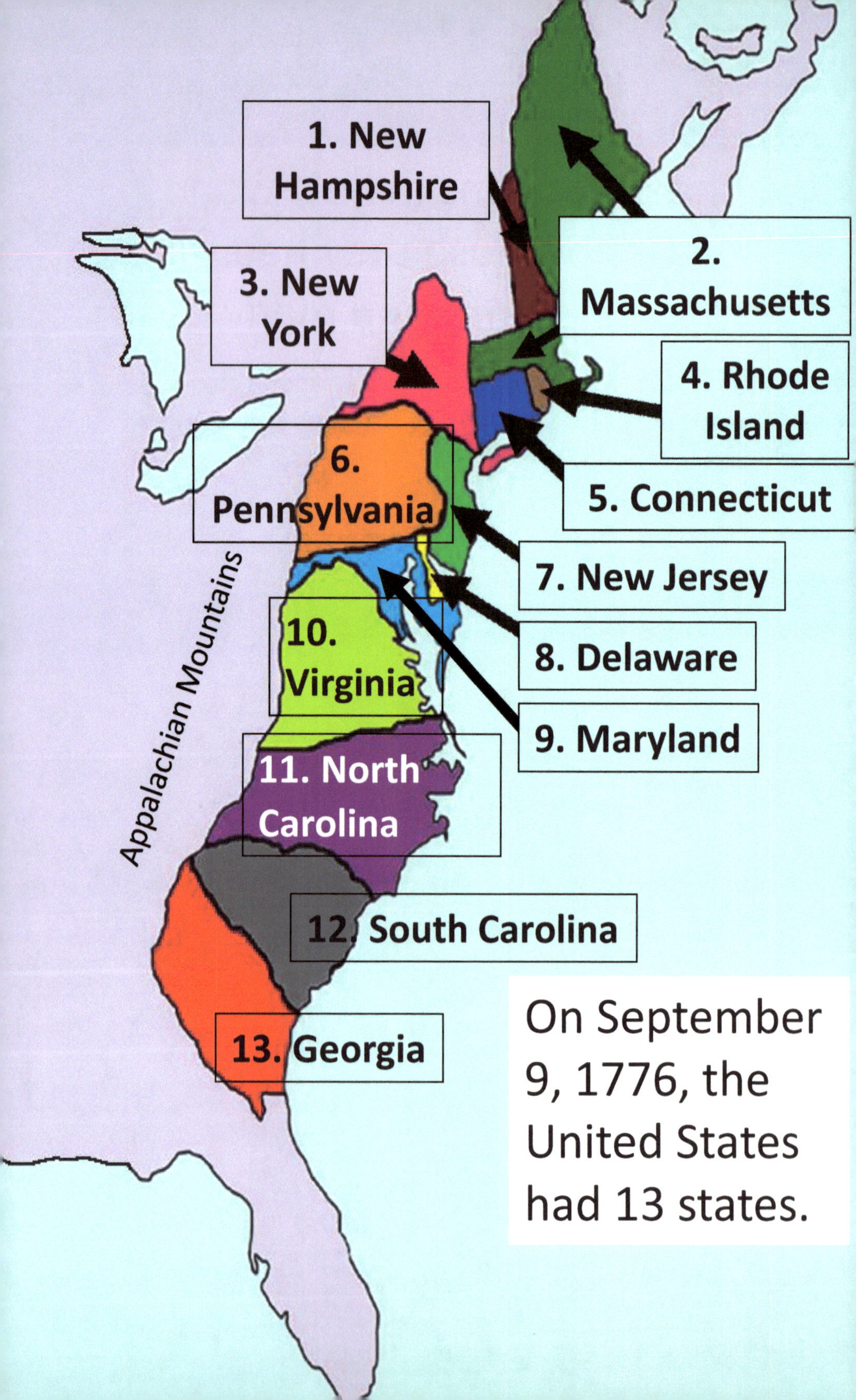

1. New Hampshire
2. Massachusetts
3. New York
4. Rhode Island
5. Connecticut
6. Pennsylvania
7. New Jersey
8. Delaware
9. Maryland
10. Virginia
11. North Carolina
12. South Carolina
13. Georgia
Appalachian Mountains
On September 9, 1776, the United States had 13 states.

For hundreds of years the high Appalachian (app-uh-LATCH-un) or (app-uh-LAY-shun) Mountains served as a barrier to western expansion.

In 1803, President Thomas Jefferson purchased the Louisiana (lew-ee-zee-ANN-uh) Territory from France for $15 million and doubled the size of the United States.

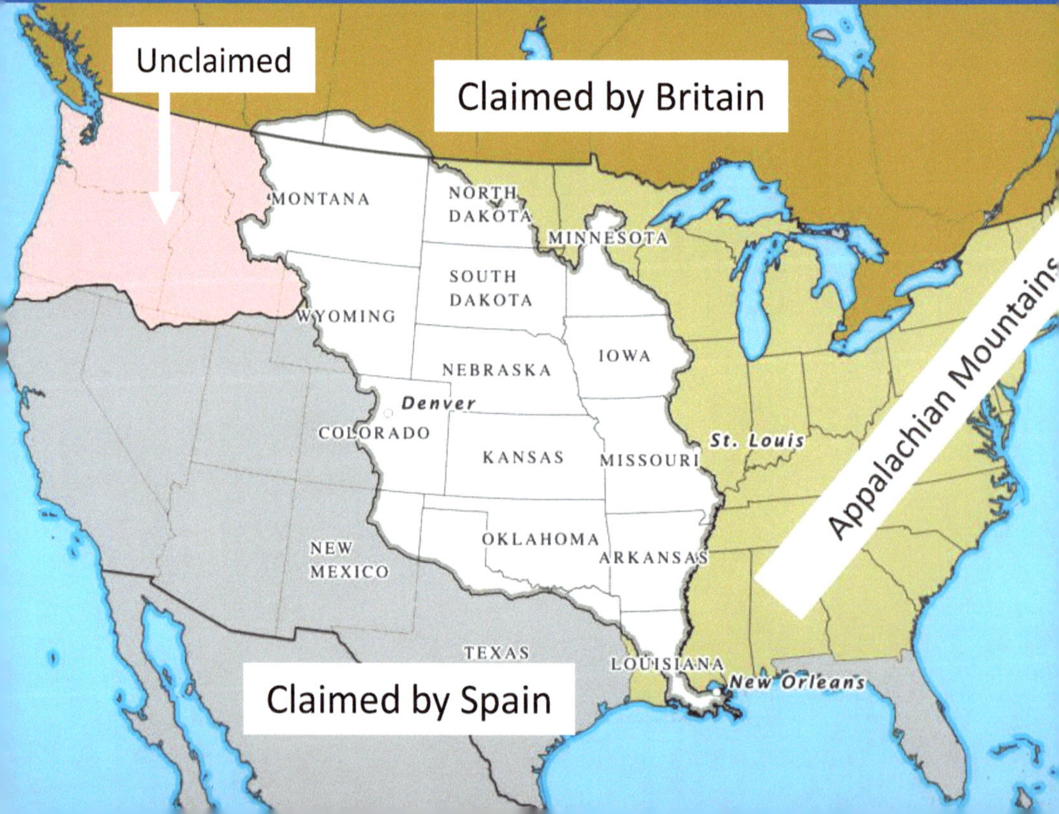

President Thomas Jefferson chose Lewis and Clark to explore the Louisiana Purchase, draw maps, keep journals, and make friends with the Native Americans.

Meriwether Lewis

William Clark

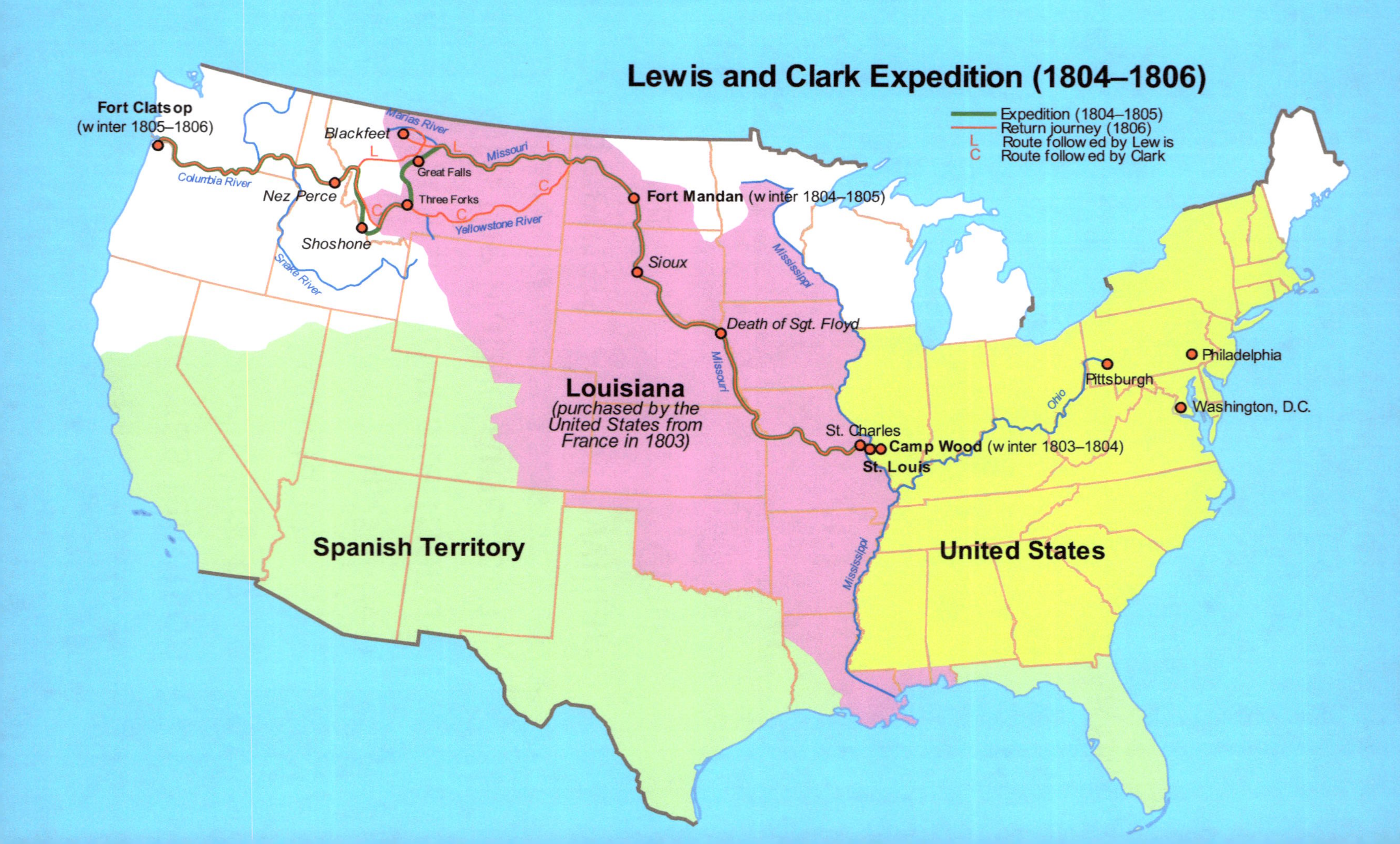

Lewis and Clark Expedition (1804–1806)
Expedition (1804–1805)
Return journey (1806)
L   Route followed by Lewis
C   Route followed by Clark
Fort Clatsop (winter 1805–1806)
Blackfeet
Great Falls
Three Forks
Nez Perce
Shoshone
Fort Mandan (winter 1804–1805)
Sioux
Death of Sgt. Floyd
Louisiana (purchased by the United States from France in 1803)
St. Charles
Camp Wood (winter 1803–1804)
St. Louis
Spanish Territory
United States
Pittsburgh
Philadelphia
Washington, D.C.
Columbia River
Snake River
Marias River
Missouri
Yellowstone River
Mississippi
Ohio

Lewis and Clark met Sacagawea (sak-uh-juh-WEE-uh) in North Dakota. She taught them about the animals and plants in different areas and helped them make contact with the Native Americans.

Led by Sacagawea, Lewis and Clark reach a Shoshone camp. The Shoshone agreed to trade horses with the group and to provide guides to lead them over the Rocky Mountains. On the difficult trip, they ran short of food. Sacagawea found and cooked roots to help the party members regain strength.

Guided by a French trapper and Sacagawea, Lewis and Clark used canoes to travel down the Columbia River to the Pacific Ocean. They had traveled 8,000 miles to the Pacific Ocean and back to St. Louis in boats, on horseback, and on foot.

The Lewis and Clark expedition started in St. Louis, Missouri. The Gateway Arch was built as a monument to the westward expansion of the United States. It is dedicated to the "American People", and is known as "The Gateway to the West".

From 1811 to 1840, fur trappers and fur traders made a trail that only had room for walking or horseback. In 1836, a wagon trail was cleared from Independence, Missouri to Fort Hall, Idaho.

The westward expansion was important in 1836 because Texas had been owned by Mexico. At the Battle of the Alamo, the Texans fought against Mexico and lost. Later in the Mexican War there would be battle cries by Texans of "Remember the Alamo!"

In 1843, the Organ Trail was completed from Independence, Missouri to Willamette, Oregon. Farmland was free to those who could make it to Oregon. Around 500,000 people walked or rode horses or rode in wagons on the Oregon Trail until 1890 when it was easier to travel by train.

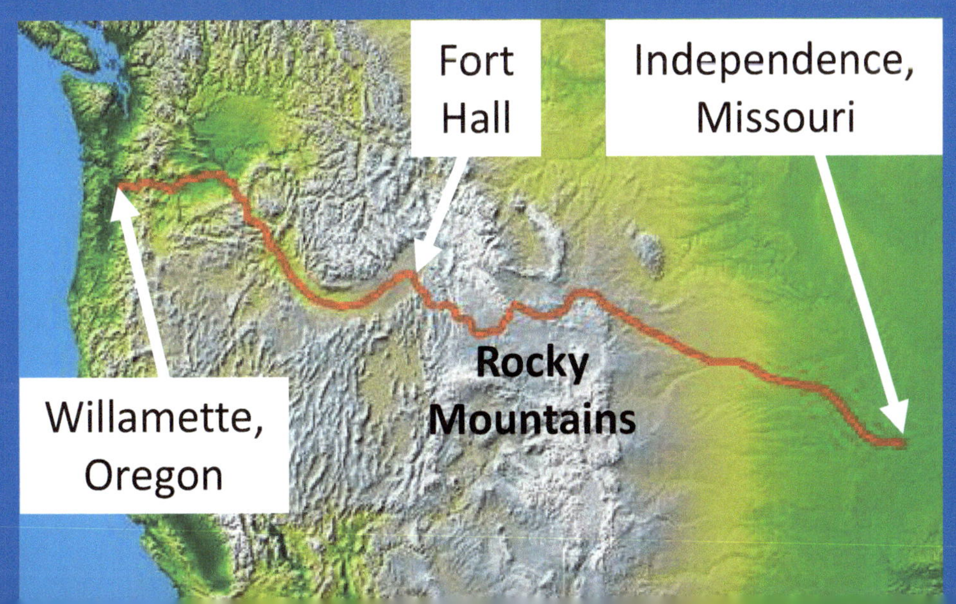

In 1845, a newspaper editor wrote about the idea that God wants the United States to expand across North America. He called it, "Manifest Destiny." The Spirit of the Frontier would guide the people west.

During the Mexican-American War (1846 - 1848), Texas became a state of the United States in 1845.
Claimed Territory
UNITED STATES
TEXAS
MEXICO

In 1848, the United States won the present-day states of Arizona (AZ), Nevada (NV), California (CA), Utah (UT), New Mexico (NM), and Texas (TX) plus parts of Colorado (CO), Kansas (KS), Wyoming (WY) and Oklahoma (OK).

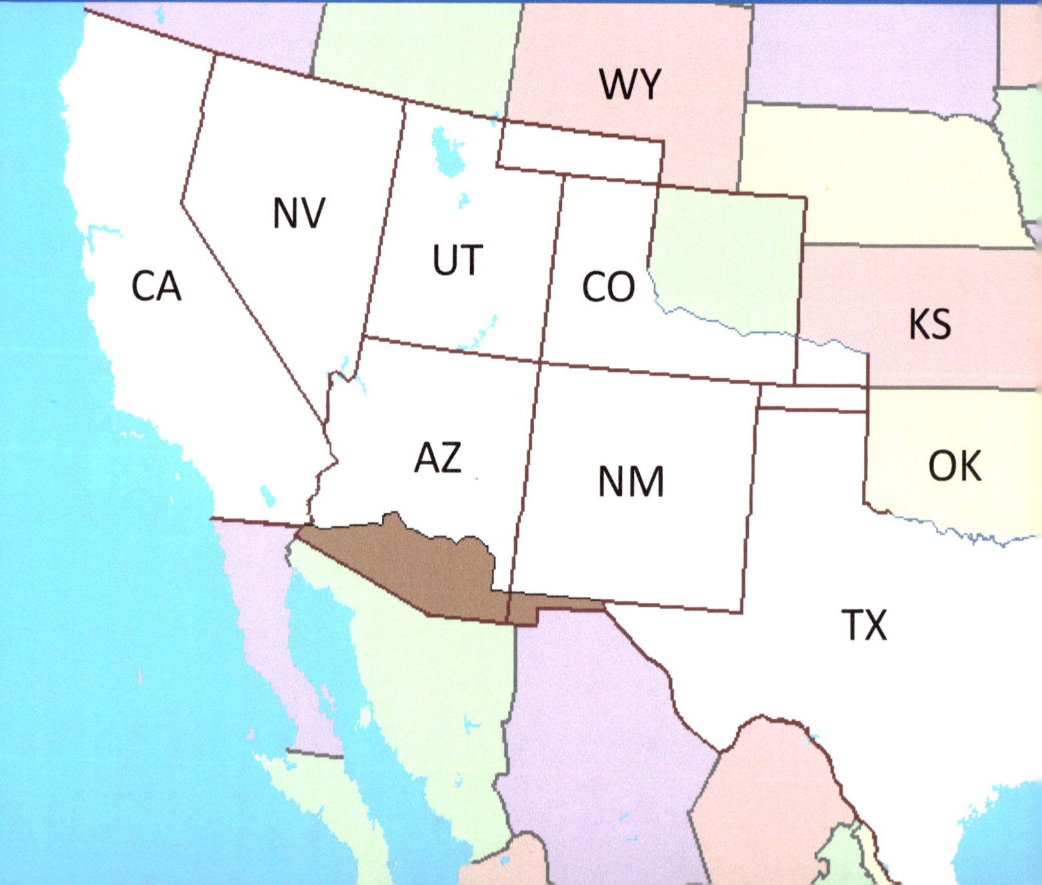

Gold would be discovered in California in 1848 leading one year later to Americans going west in the forty-niner's gold rush.

Between 1860 and 1861, the Pony Express was a relay of horse riders that carried mail from Missouri to California. The telegraph and trains later replaced it.

In 1862, to encourage families to settle the western states, land was given away for free. You had to live on it and improve the land for five years. Many people live in huts made of rooted grass (sod) because they could not afford to buy wood or stone to build a cabin.

One of the causes of the United States Civil War (1861-1864) was the Southern States wanted to have slavery in the new western states. The Northern States did not want slavery in the west. The Northern States won.

The United States moved further west with the purchase of Alaska from Russia for $7.2 million in 1867. Alaska is about twice the size of the state of Texas. There are more than three million lakes in Alaska. Alaska became a state on January 3, 1959.

From 1863 to 1869, a train route was built that connected the eastern states with the western states. The ceremony included driving a golden spike at the completion of the train line.

In 1898, Hawaii became a part of the United States. Hawaii became the 50th state on August 21, 1959.

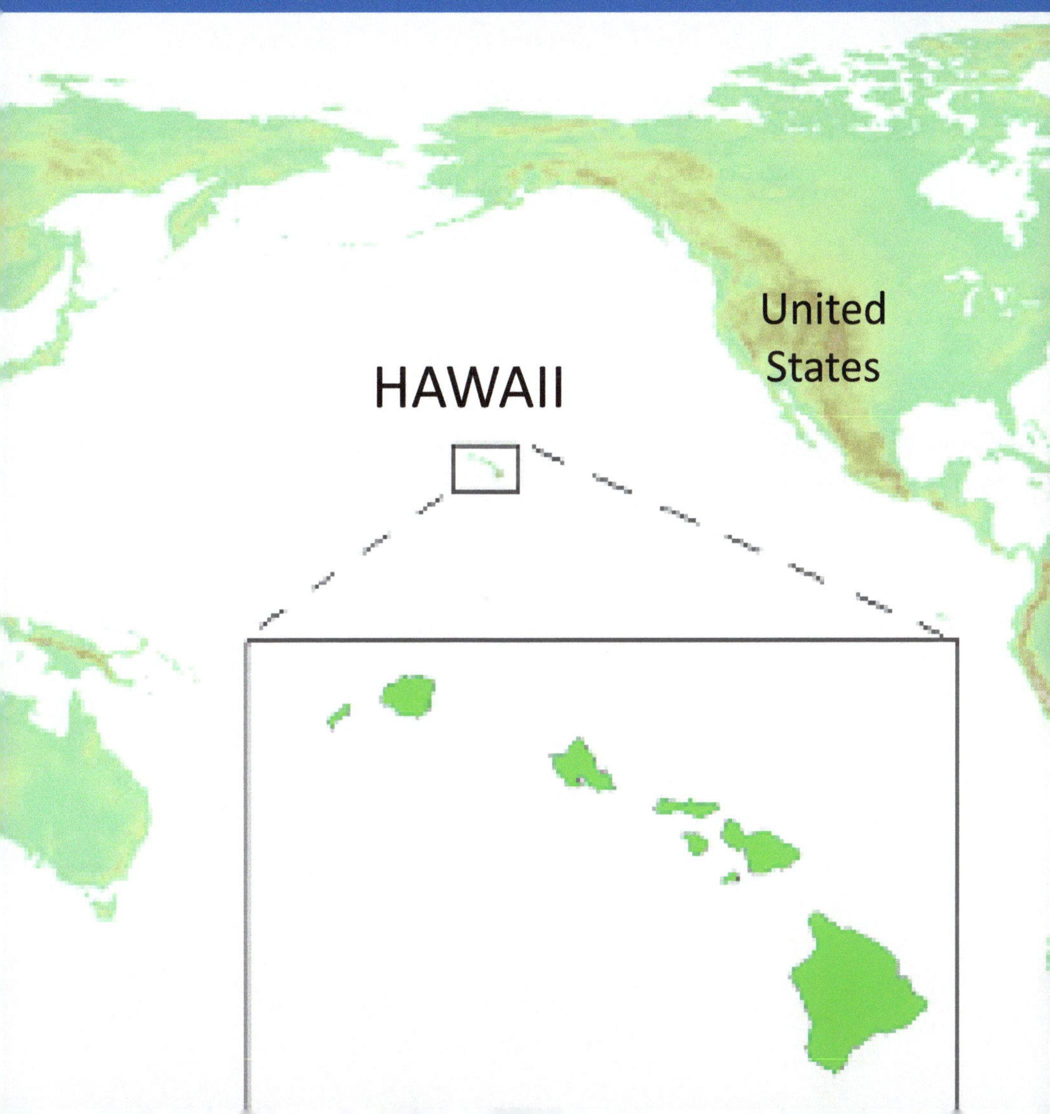

PROS and CONS of the United States Westward Movement (Manifest Destiny)

CONS

#1. Native Americans had their land taken away and were enslaved or killed.

#2. A Civil War occurred between the Northern States and the Southern States.

#3. It was against the laws of the U.S. Constitution.

#4. Can you think of other cons for the U.S. Manifest Destiny?

PROS and CONS of the United States Westward Movement (Manifest Destiny)

PROS

#1. The United States had more land for farming.
#2. Many different people added to the American Dream of a good life.
#3. The U.S. would become one of the most powerful countries in the world.
#4. Can you think of other pros for the U.S. Manifest Destiny?

Dedicated to my lovely wife Sulastri and my grandchildren Mia and Kai as well as everyone who enjoys reading about history.

For over 40 years, I have enjoyed teaching at elementary, high school and college levels. Please visit my page at Amazon.com/author/richlinville

Illustrations from OpenClipArt, PixaBay, Wiki, and illustrations purchased from Edu-Clips.

Please check out my other books at bookstores and online under the name Rich Linville.

My Alaskan Race
by Huskie Dog

Written by Rich Linville

My Basketball Blues

from the
Basketball's
Point of View
Written by Rich Linville

My Rocky Adventure!
By Rocky Magma
Written by Rich Linville

Someday I'd like to be
a rock instead of magma

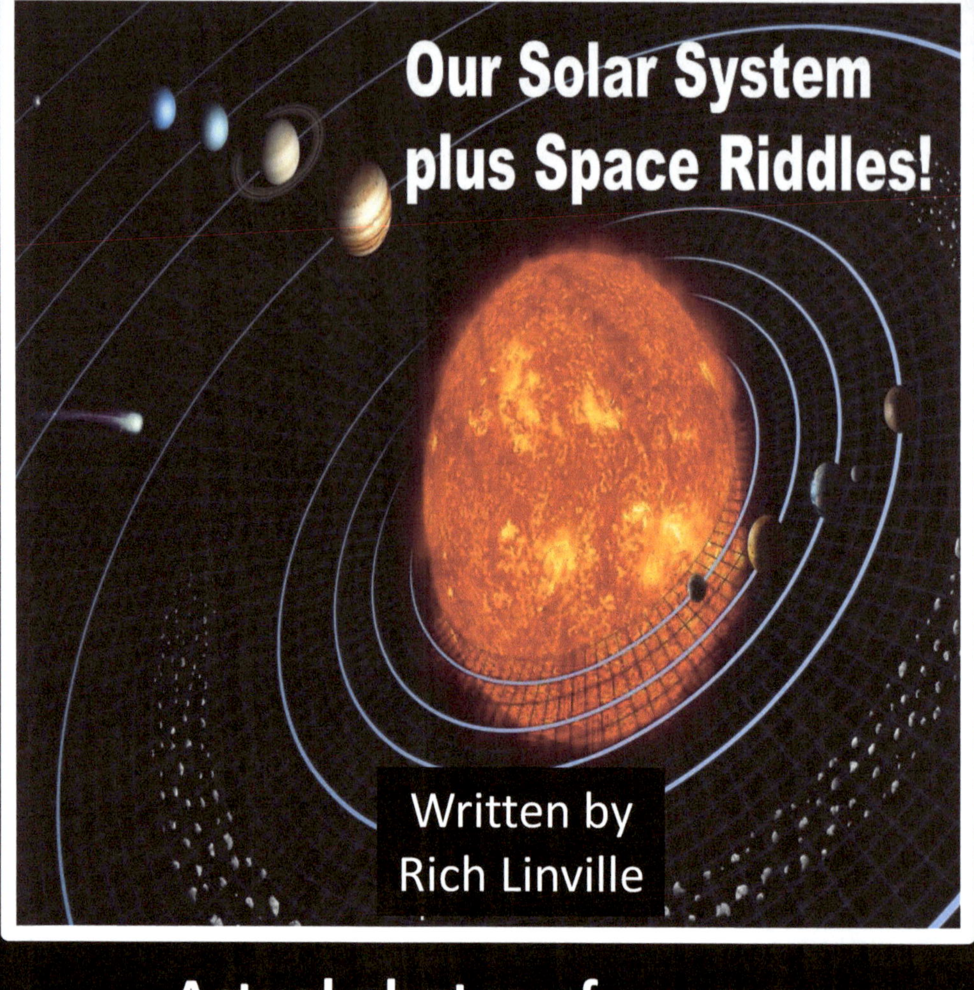

Actual photos of our sun, planets and a dwarf planet. Learn about our solar system with a trick to remember the order of the